My f Book

by Jane Belk Moncure

illustrated by Linda Hohag

THE CHILD'S WORLD

ELGIN, ILLINOIS 60120

**Library of Congress Cataloging in Publication Data**

Moncure, Jane Belk.
　My "f" book.

　(My first steps to reading)
　Rev. ed. of: My f sound box. © 1977.
　Summary: Little f puts fish, frogs, a fir tree,
flowers, and a fox in her box before having further
adventures at a farmhouse fire.
　1. Children's stories, American.　[1. Alphabet]
I. Hohag, Linda. ill.　II. Moncure, Jane Belk.　My f
sound box.　III. Title.　IV. Series: Moncure, Jane
Belk.　My first steps to reading.
PZ7.M739Myf　1984　　　　[E]　　　　84-17546
ISBN 0-89565-280-3

Distributed by Childrens Press, 1224 West Van Buren Street,
Chicago, Illinois 60607.

# My "f" Book

(Blends are included in this book.)

Little  had a box.

It was a brown box.

She said, "I will fill my  box."

Little  f found a fishing pole.

She caught

four fish.

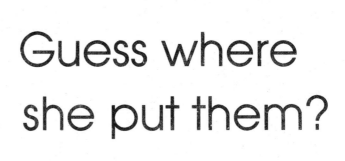

box

Guess where
she put them?

8

Then she caught five fat frogs.

"In you go," she said.

Little f found

fir trees.

She put a fir tree into her box.

"I will leave the other fir trees
in the forest," she said.

Then she
found a fox.

"I will put this fox
   into my box," said Little

"What funny things I have
in my box."

Little  came to a fence.

She climbed
over the
fence...

13

# and found a field of flowers.

She filled her box with flowers.

Little  f saw a farmhouse.

A farmer ran from the farmhouse.

# "Fire! Fire!" he cried. "Help!"

"Fire! Fire!" cried Little .

Away she ran...
back through the field
of flowers,

over the fence,

through the fir forest,

and to the...

fire
station.

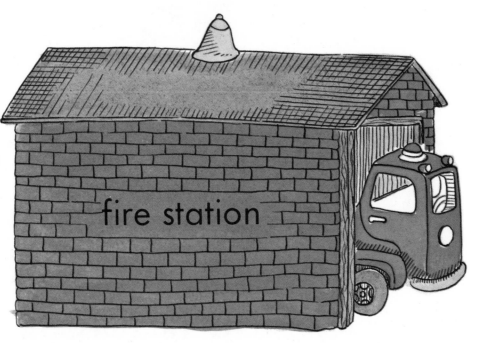

fire station

"Fire! Fire!" she cried.

"The farmhouse is on fire!"

She rang the fire 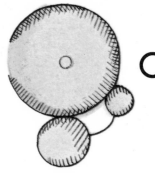 alarm.

Firemen jumped on fire engines.

Little  jumped on one too.

A fireman gave Little

a hat,

a fire hose,

boots,

and a coat.

The fire engines went fast.

The firemen
put out
the fire.

"Thank you," said the farmer.

"Thank Little ," said the firemen.
"She is our friend."

Then they took Little  back
to the fire station.

Little  f and the fox played together.

fishing pole

four fish

five fat frogs

# What fun they had.

flowers

fir tree

# More words with Little .

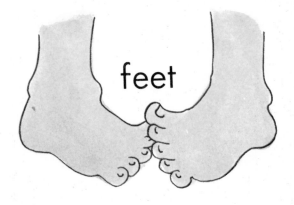
feet

fan

fork

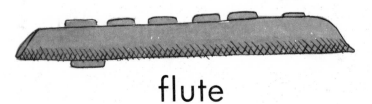
flute

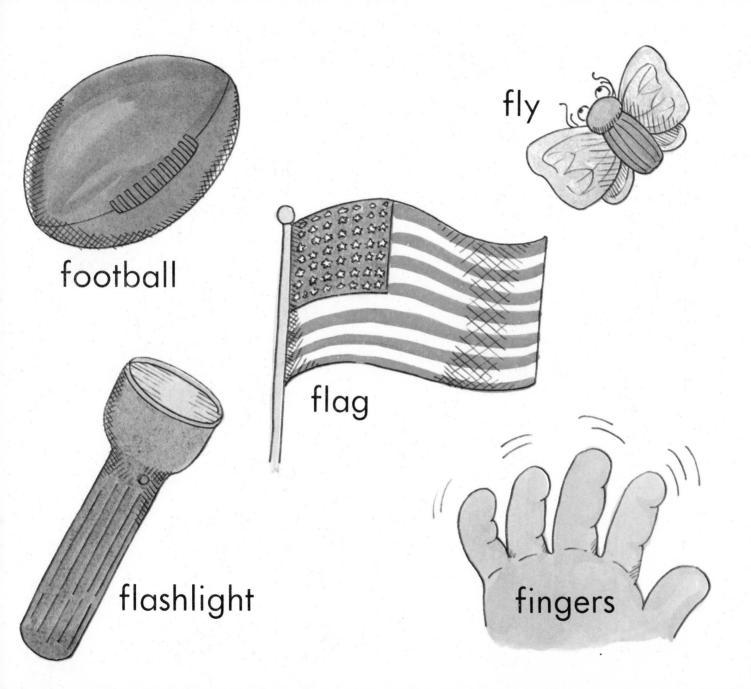

football

fly

flag

flashlight

fingers

29